# Guided Reading Notes

**Dark Red+ Band**
**Oxford Level 20**

# Into the Future

## Contents




OXFORD
UNIVERSITY PRESS

# Introduction

## Why is guided reading important?

Guided reading plays an important role in your whole-school provision for reading, providing opportunities for children to progress and develop the key competencies they need to become confident and skilled independent readers. Working with small groups of children, with texts closely matched to the readers' needs, guided reading is the perfect vehicle for delivering focused teaching from Reception/P1 right through to Year 6/P7. The teacher-pupil interaction also provides a valuable assessment opportunity, helping you identify exactly what each child can and can't do. Through guided reading children also encounter a world of exciting, whole books – building a community of readers who read for pleasure.

## About *Project X Origins*

*Project X Origins* is a comprehensive, whole-school guided reading programme designed to help you teach the wide range of skills essential to ensure children progress as readers and to help nurture a love of reading.

### Ensuring the key skills are covered

*Project X Origins* incorporates all of the key skills children need to develop to become successful and enthusiastic readers:

- **Word reading:** phonically regular and common exception words are introduced systematically in the early levels with phonic opportunities provided throughout the notes. As children progress, they are encouraged to use their decoding skills whenever they encounter new or unfamiliar words, and also to recognize how this impacts on different spelling rules.

- **Comprehension:** understanding what has been read is central to being an effective and engaged reader but comprehension is not something that comes automatically so specific strategies have been built into the notes to ensure children develop comprehension skills they can use over a range of texts:
  - Previewing
  - Predicting
  - Activating and building prior knowledge
  - Questioning
  - Recalling
  - Visualizing and other sensory responses
  - Deducting, inferring and drawing conclusions
  - Determining importance
  - Synthesizing
  - Empathizing
  - Summarizing
  - Personal response, including adopting a critical response
- **Reading fluency:** fluency occurs as children develop automatic word recognition, reading with pace and expression. Strategies to help achieve this, including meaningful opportunities for oral reading, re-reading and re-listening are provided throughout.
- **Vocabulary:** introducing new vocabulary within a meaningful context is an important element in extending children's vocabulary range, developing their reading fluency and comprehension. Each thematic cluster provides opportunities for revisiting and reinforcing vocabulary over a range of books and contexts.
- **Grammar, punctuation and spelling:** learning about language in the context of a text, rather than through a series of discrete exercises, can help make grammar, punctuation and spelling relevant and helps children make the link between grammar, punctuation and clarity of meaning, thus supporting their development as writers. Opportunities to support an in-depth look at language are provided for every book from Year 1/P2 to Year 6/P7.
- **Spoken language:** talk is crucial to learning and developing their comprehension so children are given plenty of opportunities to: discuss and debate their ideas with others; justify their opinions; ask and answer questions; explore and hypothesise; summarize, describe and explain; and listen and respond to the ideas of others.

## Assessment and progression in reading

*Project X Origins* includes a rigorous assessment spine drawn from the *Oxford Ros Wilson Reading Criterion Scale* to ensure that you know exactly what each child can do and what they need to focus on next in order to make progress. This assessment framework, combined with the careful levelling of the Oxford Levels, will help you select the right book with the right level of challenge for each of your guided reading groups and to assess, track and monitor each child's progress.

### *Step 1*

On a termly basis, use the *Reading Criterion Scale* (which can be found in the relevant *Project X Origins Teaching Handbook*) to assess each child's reading. The scale will tell you the Oxford Level a child is comfortable reading at, and the areas a child needs to develop. You can also use this assessment to form your guided reading groups.

### *Step 2*

Plan your guided reading sessions by selecting books at the appropriate Oxford Level that focus on the relevant learning needs of the group. You will find charts showing the learning objectives and assessment points for every *Project X Origins* book in the relevant *Project X Origins Teaching Handbook*. Depending on your assessment, you might choose a book at the level the children are comfortable at or one from the next level up, to offer some stretch.

### *Step 3*

Use the assessment points within the Guided Reading Notes to support on-going assessment of children's reading progress. The Progress Tracking Charts in the relevant *Project X Origins Teaching Handbook* can be used to record this if you wish. Regularly re-assess each child's progress combining your on-going informal assessments and the termly assessment using the *Reading Criterion Scale*. Use this information to re-organize guided reading groups and teaching plans in response to children's varying degrees of progress.

# Getting started: using the Guided Reading Notes

## At a glance

*Project X Origins* Guided Reading Notes offer detailed guidance to help deliver effective and engaging guided reading sessions, and are designed to be used flexibly to ensure you get the most out of each book. For notes containing multiple sessions, you may choose to focus on each of these sessions or focus on one session and have the children read the rest of the book independently.

## Curricula correlation and assessment

At the beginning of every set of notes there are correlation charts for all UK curricula, ensuring that across the clusters the main curricula objectives are covered. In addition, an overview of assessment points for each book is provided – these points are also signposted throughout the notes.

## Key information

Before the first session, an overview of the book and the resources you will need (such as additional photocopy masters) is provided.

## Teaching sequence

Each guided reading session follows the same teaching sequence:

- **Before reading**: children explore the context of each book to support their understanding and help them engage with the text. They are encouraged to discuss, recall, respond, predict and speculate about the book. Opportunities to focus on word reading and/or vocabulary are also introduced at this point.
- **During reading**: children are given a section of the book to read with specific questions in mind.
- **After reading**: children reflect on and discuss what they have read. They are encouraged to delve deeper, exploring their understanding of the text, developing their vocabulary, grammar, punctuation, spelling and fluency where appropriate.
- **Follow-up**: opportunities for children to extend their learning outside the session are provided, including writing and cross-curricular activities.

Throughout the sessions, the key strategies that children are developing are clearly identified.

# Time Trip

BY J. A. HENDERSON

## Curricula correlation

### English National Curriculum

| | |
|---|---|
| Spoken language | Give well-structured descriptions and explanations |
| Word reading | Apply their knowledge of root words, prefixes and suffixes (morphology and etymology), both to read aloud and to understand the meaning of new words that they meet |
| Comprehension | Identify how language, structure and presentation contribute to meaning |
| | Predict what might happen from details stated and implied |
| | Discuss and evaluate how authors use language, including figurative language, considering the impact on the reader |
| | Check that the text makes sense to them, discussing their understanding and exploring the meaning of words in context |

### *Developing grammar, punctuation, vocabulary and spelling*

| | | |
|---|---|---|
| Grammar and Punctuation | Expanded noun phrases to convey complicated information concisely | the world's Colleum reserves, avenue of metallic trees, dark ominous building |
| Vocabulary and Spelling | Words ending with *-ent* and *-ant* | equipment, silent, moment, basement, dormant, distant |
| | Challenge and context words | desolate, emit, perilously, smouldering, shale, forth, murk, excruciating, obliterating, engulf, consciousness, gingerly, apprehensively, hesitantly, viable, exploit, ore, frenziedly, dejectedly, ascertain, imperative, derailed, malevolent, vivid, flora, fauna, amidst, tantalized, incalcuable, console |

### *Reading assessment points*

| | |
|---|---|
| Word reading | Can the children read a range of level-appropriate texts fluently and accurately? |
| Comprehension | Can the children give detailed insight into how the structural choices support the writer's theme or purpose? |
| | Can the children infer and deduce messages, moods, feelings and attitudes, and reference ideas in the text? |
| | Can the children summarize information from different points in the same text or across a range of texts? |
| | Can the children reflect on the wider consequences or significance of information, ideas or events on the text as a whole? |

## Scottish Curriculum for Excellence

| | |
|---|---|
| Listening and talking objectives | I can select ideas and relevant information, organise these in an appropriate way for my purpose and use suitable vocabulary for my audience LIT 2-06a |
| Reading objectives | Through developing my knowledge of context clues, punctuation, grammar and layout, I can read unfamiliar texts with increasing fluency, understanding and expression ENG 2-12a / ENG 3-12a / ENG 4-12a |
| | I can select and use a range of strategies and resources before I read, and as I read, to make meaning clear and give reasons for my selection LIT 2-13a |
| | To show my understanding, I can respond to literal, inferential and evaluative questions and other close reading tasks and can create different kinds of questions of my own ENG 2-17a |

## Welsh National Literacy Framework

| | |
|---|---|
| Speaking | Speak clearly, using formal language and varying expression, tone and volume, to keep listeners interested |
| Listening | Respond to others with questions and comments which focus on reasons, implications and next steps |
| Collaboration and discussion | Contribute purposefully to group discussion to achieve agreed outcomes |
| Reading strategies | Use a range of strategies to make meaning from words and sentences, including knowledge of phonics, word roots, word families, syntax, text organisation and prior knowledge of context |
| Comprehension | Infer ideas which are not explicitly stated, e.g. writers' viewpoints or attitudes |
| Response and analysis | Consider whether text is effective in conveying information and ideas |

## Northern Ireland Curriculum

| | |
|---|---|
| Talking and Listening | Share, respond to and evaluate ideas, arguments and points of view and use evidence or reason to justify opinions, actions or proposals |
| Reading | Consider, interpret and discuss texts, exploring the ways in which language can be manipulated in order to affect the reader or engage attention |
| | Reconsider their initial response to texts in the light of insight and information which emerge subsequently from their reading |

# Session 1 (Chapters 1–2)

**About this book**

After a narrow escape on a mission to a volcano, Cat is forced to stay back at NICE HQ with an injured ankle. Little does she realise that she's about to travel somewhere far stranger ...

**You will need**

- *Between sessions*, *Character study* and *It's the future* Photocopy Masters for Year 6/P7

## Before reading

- Ask the children what the title of the book might mean. Could it be interpreted in different ways? Have they read any previous Project X books in which the team have travelled in time? What happened in them? **(recall, building on prior knowledge)**
- Read the opening paragraph together. Ask the children to make a prediction about what might happen, using other stories they have read to support this. **(predicting)**
- How might the different members of the team feel about the 'unusual readings' Dani detects? **(predicting, building on prior knowledge)**

## During reading

- Ask the children to read Chapters 1 and 2 independently.
- Ask them to note words ending in *-ant* and *-ent* as they read.

## After reading

***Returning to the text***

- Share children's questions about the text. Discuss as a group, drawing out some of the key mysteries, e.g. the two mysterious dots on Dani's monitor. How might these mysteries be linked? How do the children think Cat escaped the lava? Challenge the children to justify their opinions. **(deducing, drawing conclusions)**
- Discuss the importance of the ash cloud. Why does the author keep Cat's rescuers hidden? **(inferring)**

### *Developing comprehension*

- In pairs, ask the children to retell the moment Cat is pulled through the X-gate, one as a third-person narrator and the other in the first-person as Cat. How does this difference in perspective affect the story? What are the advantages and disadvantages of each approach? Has the author chosen the most effective voice for this scene? **(summarizing, emphasizing)** «
- Ask the children to discuss how Cat would be feeling at the different points in these chapters.

**Assessment point**
Can the children give detailed insight into how the structural choices support the writer's theme or purpose?

### *The author's craft*

- Ask the children to find an example of where direct speech is used to drive the action in the story, e.g. on page 5, "*We need to keep going Max; it's gaining on us,*" *Cat yelled*. Discuss the effect of this.

### *Developing grammar, punctuation and spelling*

- Look together at the words ending in *-ant* and *-ent*. Try to think of different ways to remember the spellings.

**Prior to Session 2**

- Ask the children to read Chapters 3 and 4 independently.
- Ask them to make notes on the *Between sessions* Photocopy Master to answer the questions about what they have read.

# Session 2 (Chapters 5–6)

## Before reading

- Share the children's responses to the questions in *Between sessions*. Remind the children to build on each other's answers, challenging ideas and opinions where appropriate.

## During reading

- Ask the children to read Chapters 5 and 6 independently.
- As they read, ask them to consider the relationship between the twins Neko and Aarek, collecting supporting evidence from the text. **(inferring, deducing, drawing conclusions)**.

**Assessment point**
Can the children read a range of level-appropriate texts fluently and accurately?

## After reading

***Returning to the text***

Ask the children:

- Will Cat be able to keep what she has seen in the future a secret? What evidence is there in the text that she will? (Her letter to Neko) **(recall, predicting)**
- What motivated Aarek to take the e-device? **(emphasizing)**

### *Developing comprehension*

- Cat says in her letter that knowing too much about the future could *change the course of history beyond our comprehension* (p.33). What might be dangerous about her learning about the future? **(deducing, inferring, drawing conclusions)**

**Assessment point**
Can the children infer and deduce messages, moods, feelings and attitudes, and reference ideas in the text?

### *Developing grammar, punctuation and spelling*

- Ask the children to find the phrase *the world's Colleum reserves* on page 33. Check the group understand the meaning of the phrase (all the Colleum that exists in the world). Revise how expanded noun phrases, such as this, can be useful for providing detail in a concise way. Ask the children to note down other expounded noun phrases in the text, e.g. *their owner's genetic profile* (p.32).

**Prior to Session 3**

- Ask the children to read Chapters 7 and 8 independently.
- Ask them to make notes about Aarek on the *Character study* Photocopy Master.

# Session 3 (Chapters 9–12)

## Before reading

- Share the children's responses to the character study task. Challenge children to extend and justify their answers.
- Ask the children to look back at their original questions from Session 1. Which questions can they now answer? Do they have any new questions to add?

## During reading

- Ask the children to read Chapters 9–12 independently, noting any vocabulary ending with *-ough*.

## After reading

### *Returning to the text*

- Can the children list all of the places and times in the book? Challenge the children to devise a visual way of recording this (e.g. as a diagram, graph or picture).

**Assessment point**
Can the children summarize information from different points in the same text or across a range of texts?

### *Developing comprehension*

- As a group, re-read the final paragraph of page 59. Ask the children to summarize what has happened, allowing them to look back at different points in the story. Then ask them to look back at their original questions from Session 1 – does this ending help to answer them? **(summarizing, synthesizing)**

### *The author's craft*

- Can the children think of elements in the story where an idea is returned to later in the story (Cat being rescued, Neko's hoverboard)? What is the effect of this on the reader?
- When Cat is dragged through the X-gate, the author uses the pronoun 'her' rather than 'Cat'. How does the author use pronouns in this last section to prolong the mystery?

**Assessment point**
Can the children reflect on the wider consequences or significance of information, ideas or events on the text as a whole?

### Developing grammar, punctuation and spelling

- Ask the children to share the examples of *-ough* words they collected and categorize them in lists according to the sound of their endings. Can they think of ways to remember the spelling of the different words it appears in?

## Follow-up

*Writing activities*

- Rewrite the part of the story where Cat and Neko are chasing Aarek from *his* point of view. **(longer writing task)**
- Write the letter Cat leaves for Neko explaining what has happened. Remember, Cat doesn't tell Neko the whole story! **(short writing task)**

*Other literacy activities*

- As a group, list the technological devices in the story (capsule, XZ300 motorized boots, etc.). In pairs, give the children three minutes to plan a 'pitch' (using *It's the future* Photocopy Master) about why theirs is the most valuable technological advance to present to the group.
- As a group, skim read Chapter 7, discussing Aarek's character and his motivation for taking the e-device. Ask the children to imagine Aarek is caught and has to appear in court. In pairs, ask the children to take the role of lawyers: one prosecuting and one defending Aarek.
- Recommend other books about time travel such as *The Time Machine* by H G Wells or *Tom's Midnight Garden* by Philippa Pearce.

*Cross-curricular activities*

- Research volcanic eruptions. **(Geography)**
- Design a type of future transport and produce an annotated drawing of how it works. **(DT)**
- Use percussion instruments to compose music to accompany the chase scenes. **(Music)**

# A Dangerous Game

BY ANTHONY McGOWAN

## Curricula correlation

### English National Curriculum

| | |
|---|---|
| Spoken language | Consider and evaluate different viewpoints, attending to and building on the contributions of others |
| Word reading | Apply their knowledge of root words, prefixes and suffixes (morphology and etymology), both to read aloud and to understand the meaning of new words that they meet |
| Comprehension | Discuss and evaluate how authors use language, including figurative language, considering the impact on the reader |
| | Identify how language, structure and presentation contribute to meaning |
| | Draw inferences and justify these with evidence from the text |

***Developing grammar, punctuation, vocabulary and spelling***

| | | |
|---|---|---|
| Grammar and Punctuation | Use of modal verbs to indicate degrees of possibility | everything *will* be back to normal; usually they *would* reappear; I'm glad you *could* make it |
| Vocabulary and Spelling | Endings spelt *-cious* and *-tious* | suspicious, ferocious, cautious |
| | Challenge and context words | commotion, ice stack, shards, perplexed, peppering, genetics, irregular, conundrum, remit, preposterous, malfunctioning, space-time continuum, dismayed, violation, disqualification, piqued, formula, theoretical, devised, anomaly, fluctuation |

***Reading assessment points***

| | |
|---|---|
| Word reading | Can the children read a range of level-appropriate texts fluently and accurately? |
| Comprehension | Can the children reflect on the wider consequences or significance of information, ideas or events on the text as a whole? |
| | Can the children securely make deductions, firmly rooted in the evidence in the text? |
| | Can the children explain in detail how the author has used different language features? |
| | Can the children summarize information from different points in the same text or across a range of texts? |
| | Can the children infer and deduce messages, moods, feelings and attitudes, and reference ideas in the text? |
| | Can the children use quotations and text references to support ideas and arguments? |

## Scottish Curriculum for Excellence

| | |
|---|---|
| Listening and talking objectives | When listening and talking with others for different purposes, I can share information, experiences and opinions LIT 2-09a |
| Reading objectives | Through developing my knowledge of context clues, punctuation, grammar and layout, I can read unfamiliar texts with increasing fluency, understanding and expression ENG 2-12a / ENG 3-12a / ENG 4-12a |
| | To show my understanding across different areas of learning, I can identify and consider the purpose and main ideas of a text and use supporting detail LIT 2-16a |
| | I can discuss structure, characterisation and/or setting ENG 2-19a |

## Welsh National Literacy Framework

| | |
|---|---|
| Speaking | Speak clearly, using formal language and varying expression, tone and volume, to keep listeners interested |
| Listening | Respond to others with questions and comments which focus on reasons, implications and next steps |
| Collaboration and discussion | Contribute purposefully to group discussion to achieve agreed outcomes |
| Reading strategies | Use a range of strategies to make meaning from words and sentences, including knowledge of phonics, word roots, word families, syntax, text organisation and prior knowledge of context |
| Comprehension | Show understanding of main ideas and significant details in different texts on the same topic |
| Response and analysis | Consider whether text is effective in conveying information and ideas |

## Northern Ireland Curriculum

| | |
|---|---|
| Talking and Listening | Tell, retell and interpret stories based on memories, personal experiences, literature, imagination and the content of the curriculum |
| Reading | Justify their responses logically, by inference, deduction and/or reference to evidence within the text, for example, compare and contrast two characters in a story or history text |
| | Use a range of cross-checking strategies to read unfamiliar words in texts |

# Session 1 (Chapters 1 and 2)

**About this book**

After their watches malfunction, Team X find themselves on an enforced break. A mysterious email leads Ant into danger and Team X attempts to rescue him.

**You will need**

- *Character study* and *Typing errors* Photocopy Masters for Year 6/P7

## Before reading

- Discuss the title together. What might it mean? What might happen to Team X? **(predicting)**
- From reading the back cover blurb, who do they think will be the key protagonist in the story? (Ant) Discuss what they know about Ant as a character and how they think this might shape the story. **(building on prior knowledge, predicting)**

## During reading

- Ask the children to read Chapters 1 and 2 independently.
- As they read, ask the children to make a list of modal verbs (would, could, will, can, might).

## After reading

***Returning to the text***

Ask the children:

- What was odd about Dani's glass smashing? Did you pay much attention to this when it first happened? **(recall, inferring)**
- What was wrong with the team's watches? What would be the significance of Team X losing their watches? **(deducing)**

***Developing comprehension***

- Return to page 6, re-reading the two paragraphs where the glass is mentioned. Ask the children what the reader learns about the significance of the glass breaking in Chapter 2. Can the group think of other stories where small, seemingly insignificant clues turn out to be very important?

**Assessment point**

Can the children reflect on the wider consequences or significance of information, ideas or events on the text as a whole?

### The author's craft

- Ask the children to skim through Chapters 1 and 2, adding notes to *Character study* Photocopy Master. What do we know about Tiger from his actions and speech? How does this compare to when the author directly describes a character? Is it an effective way of giving the reader information about a character?

### Developing grammar, punctuation and spelling

- Look at the list of modal verbs the children found. Discuss how modal verbs tell a reader how likely something is to happen. Experiment with exchanging one modal verb for another in each sentence. How does it affect the meaning?

**Prior to Session 2**

- Ask the children to read Chapters 3–5 independently.
- As they read, ask them to collect clues or hints that they think might turn out to be important later in the story.

# Session 2 (Chapter 6 and 7)

## Before reading

- In pairs, recap the story so far.
- As a group, consider the clues the children have collected. Which clues do the children agree will be significant? Discuss the email Ant received and the fact that *it was almost as if the questions had been devised especially for him* (p.16).

**Assessment point**
Can the children securely make deductions, firmly rooted in the evidence in the text?

## During reading

- Ask the children to read Chapters 6 and 7 independently.
- Ask them to record unfamiliar or challenging words they notice.

## After reading

### *Returning to the text*

Ask the children:

- Where does Tiger's watch take him in Chapter 7? **(recall, inferring)**
- How do you think Ant could eventually become the Collector's assistant? Challenge the children to imagine and describe the gradual process. Will this future definitely come true? How might it be avoided? **(visualizing, predicting)**
- Return to the clues the children collected. Are there any that have proved to be important? Might any clues explain how Ant could work with the Collector?

### *Developing comprehension*

- Ask the children to identify what the italicized text on pages 27 and 30 is. (The characters' thoughts). What is the effect of including these? How else could the thoughts be conveyed? (Through the narrator's voice.) How would this change the effect?

**Assessment point**

Can the children explain in detail how the author has used different language features?

- In pairs, ask the children to take it in turns to re-read one paragraph from the story aloud, with a partner adding a thought-track as the action happens. **(empathizing)**
- Ask the children to write down the characters' thoughts at various points in the story. **(empathizing)**

### *Developing vocabulary*

- Return to the lists of challenging words the children made. As a group, clarify the meanings. Where possible, draw their attention to how morphology (root words, prefixes and suffixes) and etymology (origin of words) can help them to work out meanings and spelling.

**Prior to Session 3**

- Ask the children to read Chapters 8–10 independently.
- Ask them to look for any changes in Ant's character as they read, noting how the author shares this with the reader.

# Session 3 (Chapters 11–13)

## Before reading

- Allocate a character from the book to each child and ask the group to recap the story so far from their character's perspective. Encourage the children to challenge one another if they stray from their character's perspective. **(recall, summarizing, emphasizing)**
- Discuss how Ant's character has changed, based on the children's notes. **(inferring)**

## During reading

- Ask the children to read Chapters 11–13 independently.
- As they read, ask the children to make a list of words ending with *-cious* and *-tious*.

**Assessment point**
Can the children read a range of level-appropriate texts fluently and accurately?

## After reading

***Returning to the text***

Ask the children:

- Allocate a character from the book to each child and ask the group to recap the story so far from their character's perspective. Encourage the children to challenge one another if they stray from their character's perspective. **(recall, summarizing, emphasizing)**

**Assessment point**
Can the children summarize information from different points in the same text or across a range of texts?

- How does Ant feel at the end of Chapter 12? Is it possible to describe his emotions in one word or are his feelings more complicated? Can the children find examples from the text to justify their opinions? **(empathizing)**

**Assessment point**
Can the children infer and deduce messages, moods, feelings and attitudes, and reference ideas in the text?

### Developing comprehension

- Divide the group into two teams and give each one a side of the argument: Should Team X tell Ant about what Tiger saw in the future? Encourage the children to draw on evidence from this book and their knowledge of the characters to support their argument. How might telling or not telling Ant affect the future?

**Assessment point**
Can the children use quotations and text references to support ideas and arguments?

### Developing grammar, punctuation and spelling

- Look at the words the children listed ending in *-cious* and *-tious*, noting the different spellings. Explain that it can be difficult to know which ending to use. A rule to remember is that if the root word ends in *-ce* then *-cious* will be used (fierce/ferocious). In pairs, challenge the children to think of as many other words as they can using these letter-strings.

## Follow-up

### *Writing activities*

- Write a letter of apology from Ant to Dani Day and the rest of Team X for betraying them. Challenge the children to elaborate and list Ant's reasons for his actions. **(longer writing task)**
- Ask the children to write a short first-person narrative where they travel to the future. **(shorter writing task)**

### *Other literacy activities*

- Ask the children to correct Ant's email on the *Typing errors* Photocopy Master.
- Write Rodney Grape's diary about the *Scientist of the Future.*

### *Cross-curricular activities*

- Research and write test questions for Ant to answer. **(Science)**
- Research mammoths and produce a fact file about them, detailing how they evolved to match their habitat and lifestyle. **(Science/Computing)**

# After Tomorrow

BY GILLIAN CROSS

## Curricula correlation

### English National Curriculum

| | |
|---|---|
| Spoken language | Articulate and justify answers, arguments and opinions |
| Word reading | Apply their knowledge of root words, prefixes and suffixes (morphology and etymology), both to read aloud and to understand the meaning of new words that they meet |
| Comprehension | Draw inferences such as inferring characters' feelings, thoughts and motives from their actions, and justifying inferences with evidence |
| | Predict what might happen from details stated and implied |
| | Provide reasoned justifications for their views |

### *Developing grammar, punctuation, vocabulary and spelling*

| | | |
|---|---|---|
| Grammar and Punctuation | Use of the question tag to show structures typical of informal speech | Range of purposes in Chapter 1 |
| Vocabulary and Spelling | Words with the letter strings *-ibly* and *-ably* | miserably, probably, terribly, horribly, incredibly |
| | Challenge and context words | registered, chivvied, portaloos, trenches, rustler, careering, earnestly, haulage firm, insurance, obsessed, Allen keys, realigned, grovelled, plaintively, hyperdrive, frazzled, laced, freight cars, asylum, rubber-stamped, scuffling, dilapidated, spokes, indignantly |

### *Reading assessment points*

| | |
|---|---|
| Word reading | Can the children read a range of level-appropriate texts fluently and accurately? |
| Comprehension | Can the children evaluate relationships between characters? |
| | Can children clearly identify the effect the writing has on the reader, and begin to explain how this impact has been created? |
| | Can the children use quotations and text references to support ideas and arguments? |
| | Can the children give detailed insight into how the structural choices support the writer's theme or purpose? |
| | Can the children explore texts to find evidence to support their views? |

## Scottish Curriculum for Excellence

| | |
|---|---|
| Listening and talking objectives | When listening and talking with others for different purposes, I can share information, experiences and opinions LIT 2-09a |
| Reading objectives | Through developing my knowledge of context clues, punctuation, grammar and layout, I can read unfamiliar texts with increasing fluency, understanding and expression ENG 2-12a / ENG 3-12a / ENG 4-12a |
| | I can make notes, organise them under suitable headings and use them to understand information, develop my thinking, explore problems and create new texts, using my own words as appropriate LIT 2-15a |
| | I can discuss structure, characterisation and/or setting; recognise the relevance of the writer's theme and how this relates to my own and others' experiences; discuss the writer's style and other features appropriate to genre ENG 2-19a |

## Welsh National Literacy Framework

| | |
|---|---|
| Speaking | Speak clearly, using formal language and varying expression, tone and volume, to keep listeners interested |
| Listening | Respond to others with questions and comments which focus on reasons, implications and next steps |
| Collaboration and discussion | Follow up points in group discussions, showing agreement or disagreement giving reasons |
| Reading strategies | Understand how punctuation can vary and so affect sentence structure and meaning |
| Comprehension | Infer ideas which are not explicitly stated, e.g. writers' viewpoints or attitudes |
| Response and analysis | Consider whether text is effective in conveying information and ideas |

## Northern Ireland Curriculum

| | |
|---|---|
| Talking and Listening | Share, respond to and evaluate ideas, arguments and points of view and use evidence or reason to justify opinions, actions or proposals |
| Reading | Consider, interpret and discuss texts, exploring the ways in which language can be manipulated in order to affect the reader or engage attention |
| | Justify their responses logically, by inference, deduction and/or reference to evidence within the text, for example, compare and contrast two characters in a story or history text |

# Session 1 (Chapters 1 and 2)

**About this book**

Britain's economy collapses – the currency is worthless, food is in short supply and raiders roam the streets. Matt and his family, after years of struggling to survive, decide to flee to France but the life in a refugee camp proves just as testing.

**You will need**

- *Between sessions* and *Text messages* Photocopy Masters for Year 6/P7

## Before reading

- Read the opening line of the story together. Discuss how the author uses this line to draw the reader into the text. How effective is it at doing this? **(personal response)**
- From reading the blurb and considering the front cover, what do the children think will be the themes of this book? What kind of vision of the future does it present? **(predicting)**

## During reading

- Ask the children to read Chapters 1 and 2 independently.
- Allocate one member of the family in the story to each child. As they read, ask them to collect words and phrases that describe their given character.

**Assessment point**

Can the children read a range of level-appropriate texts fluently and accurately?

## After reading

### *Returning to the text*

Ask the children:

- What has happened in this version of the near future? Why is food so scarce and valuable? Challenge the group to use evidence from the text to justify their answers. **(recall, deducing, inferring, drawing conclusions)**
- Why do the raiders target Matt's family? Do they have any justification in doing so? **(deducing, inferring, personal response)**
- Ask each child to give feedback about their given character. Discuss how the author's language provides detail, both explicitly and implicitly (through words and actions, adverbs and noun phrases).

### Developing comprehension

- As a group, discuss how Matt views his father and Justin (starting with Matt's dream on page 12). How does the author use language to reinforce these different views? Do the children agree with Matt's opinion? Is Matt being fair to Justin?

**Assessment point**
Can the children evaluate relationships between characters?

### The author's craft

- Look at the last line of Chapter 2 together. Why has the author chosen to end on this line? What is the intended effect of this on the reader?

**Assessment point**
Can the children clearly identify the effect the writing has on the reader, and begin to explain how this impact has been created?

### Developing grammar, punctuation and spelling

- Turn to page 16 and point out the question tag in *'Had to get Bob on our side, didn't I?'* Remind the children that in informal speech, we often use tags at the end of questions. Ask them to find two more examples in Chapter 2, e.g. *'That's not going to last very long, is it?'* (p.14) and *'There's always more than we can eat–isn't there, Dad?'* (p.15).

**Prior to Session 2**

- Ask the children to read until the end of Chapter 12.
- Ask them to add notes to the *Between sessions* Photocopy Master.

# Session 2

## Before reading

- Ask the children to share the work they completed between sessions.
- Re-read pages 118–120 where Matt encounters the two old ladies. Why do the children think they treat him like this? What is the effect of the meeting on Matt? Challenge the children to quote from the text to justify their answers.

**Assessment point**
Can the children use quotations and text references to support ideas and arguments?

## During reading

- Ask the children to read Chapters 13 and 14 independently.
- As they read, ask them to note how each character is adapting to life in the camp and how they are choosing to use their time.

## After reading

***Returning to the text***

Ask the children:

- On page 166, why does Steff suggest that Matt fix the oldest and most damaged bike? **(deducing, inferring)**
- Has Matt changed since the start of the book? Challenge the children to use evidence from the text to justify their answers. **(personal response, synthesizing, drawing conclusions)**
- What do the children think will happen next in the story? **(predicting)**

### *Developing comprehension*

- On page 112 Salman says: '*Camps like this are always tough … the people who come through best are the people who make things happen*'. Give children time, in pairs, to discuss this statement. Which of the characters are 'making things happen'? Which ones do they think will 'come through best'? Share the children's thoughts and ask the children to record their predictions for those characters who things will end well for at the end of the book.

### *The author's craft*

- As a group, re-read the section where Matt is fixing the bicycle on page 175: *It didn't look as though anyone …* What does this tell us about Matt's character? How does the author communicate Matt's careful and deliberate nature implicitly? **(deducing, inferring)**
- Look at the last lines of Chapter 14 : *And there was a rat hanging from his thumb. Holding on by its teeth.* How does structuring this as two short sentences emphasize the drama of the situation?

**Assessment point**

Can the children give detailed insight into how the structural choices support the writer's theme or purpose?

### Developing grammar, punctuation and spelling

- Ask the children to skim through the book collecting words that end with *-ibly* and *-ably*. Ask children to list any more they can think of and spelling patterns.

**Prior to Session 3**

- Ask the children to read until the end of Chapter 22 before the next session.
- Ask them to note unfamiliar words and phrases as they read.

# Session 3

## Before reading

- Ask the children to share the words and phrases they collected during their independent reading. As a group, discuss their meanings.
- Discuss how life in the camp is different from the 'normal world'. What are the different challenges? What are the rules that govern life for the people in the camp? **(deducing, inferring, drawing conclusions, empathizing)**
- Ask each child to predict how the story will end. **(predicting)**

## During reading

- Ask the children to read the last chapter of the book independently.
- As they read, ask them to think about how the story ends for each the characters and how this matched their predictions.

## After reading

***Returning to the text***

Ask the children:

- Ask the group whether they enjoyed the story. Challenge them to comment on the themes and specific stylistic features in addition to the characters and plot. **(personal response)**

**Assessment point**

Can the children explore texts to find evidence to support their views?

### Developing comprehension

- In pairs then as a group, discuss how the author uses bikes (a recurring theme) to move the story along, to tell the reader about Matt and as a metaphor at different points in the story.

### The author's craft

- Re-read the final paragraph. What is the author suggesting by the text ... *the road that went on and on, into a whole, unknown country. If you want to stay balanced, you have to keep moving'*?
- Why does the author leave the ending open? Is this a positive ending for Matt? What is the effect of this on the reader? What else would the group like to know?

**Assessment point**
Can the children give detailed insight into how the structural choices support the writer's theme or purpose?

## Follow-up

*Writing activities*

- Write one of Salman's news reports from the camp. Challenge the children to employ a journalistic style. **(longer writing task)**
- Use the *Text messages* Photocopy Master to write the messages that Matt's mother has been sending to Bob's phone. **(short writing task)**

*Other literacy activities*

- Write a short story about where Bob goes next and what happens to him. This could be in the form of a diary.

*Cross-curricular activities*

- Visit the Red Cross website to explore issues raised by the book. **(PSHE)**
- Research the construction of the Channel Tunnel and facts around it. **(Science, DT, Mathematics, Geography)**
- Find the route of the next Tour de France and track it on a map. **(Geography)**

# Fight for the Future: Ant vs the Collector

BY PAUL MASON

## Curricula correlation

### English National Curriculum

| | |
|---|---|
| Spoken language | Give well-structured descriptions and explanations |
| Word reading | Apply their knowledge of root words, prefixes and suffixes (morphology and etymology), both to read aloud and to understand the meaning of new words that they meet |
| Comprehension | Retrieve, record and present information from non-fiction |
| | Identify how language, structure and presentation contribute to meaning |
| | Identify and discuss themes and conventions in and across a wide range of writing |

***Developing grammar, punctuation, vocabulary and spelling***

| | | |
|---|---|---|
| Grammar and Punctuation | Use of hyphens to avoid ambiguity | bio-domes, counter-attack |
| Vocabulary and Spelling | Words ending in *-able* and *-ible* | miserable, enjoyable, terrible, responsible |
| | Challenge and context words | air miles, aquifer, arable, coastal erosion, commute, congestion, degrade, desertification, extinction, fertile, hemp, ice floe, irrigation, overgrazing, petition |

***Reading assessment points***

| | |
|---|---|
| Word reading | Can the children read a range of level-appropriate texts fluently and accurately? |
| Comprehension | Can the children use quotations and text references to support ideas and arguments? |
| | Can the children identify the purpose, audience and organization of texts and evaluate the success of each of these elements? |
| | Can the children give detailed insight into how the structural choices support the writer's theme or purpose? |
| | Can the children clearly identify and retrieve relevant points and key ideas from different points in a text and across a range of texts? |
| | Can the children combine information with increasing precision to produce meaningful information? |
| | Can the children discuss the range of organizational features used and how they contribute to the overall effect of the text? |
| | Can the children clearly identify and explain the writer's viewpoint, making references to the text? |

## Scottish Curriculum for Excellence

| | |
|---|---|
| Listening and talking objectives | To help me develop an informed view, I can distinguish fact from opinion, and I am learning to recognise when my sources try to influence me and how useful these are LIT 2-08a |
| Reading objectives | Through developing my knowledge of context clues, punctuation, grammar and layout, I can read unfamiliar texts with increasing fluency, understanding and expression ENG 2-12a / ENG 3-12a / ENG 4-12a |
| | To show my understanding, I can respond to literal, inferential and evaluative questions and other close reading tasks and can create different kinds of questions of my own ENG 2-17a |
| | To help me develop an informed view, I can identify and explain the difference between fact and opinion, recognise when I am being influenced, and have assessed how useful and believable my sources are LIT 2-18a |

## Welsh National Literacy Framework

| | |
|---|---|
| Speaking | Speak clearly, using formal language and varying expression, tone and volume, to keep listeners interested |
| Listening | Listen carefully to presentations and show understanding of the speakers' conclusions or opinions |
| Collaboration and discussion | Contribute purposefully to group discussion to achieve agreed outcomes |
| Reading strategies | Use a range of strategies for finding information, e.g. skimming for gist, scanning for detail |
| Comprehension | Identify ideas and information that interest them to develop further understanding |
| Response and analysis | Distinguish between facts, theories and opinions |

## Northern Ireland Curriculum

| | |
|---|---|
| Talking and Listening | Share, respond to and evaluate ideas, arguments and points of view and use evidence or reason to justify opinions, actions or proposals |
| Reading | Justify their responses logically, by inference, deduction and/or reference to evidence within the text, for example, compare and contrast two characters in a story or history text |
| | Use a variety of reading skills for different reading purposes |

# Session 1 (pages 4–11)

**About this book**

In this non-fiction text, we explore the Collector's plan to bring environmental chaos to Earth and Team X's plan to stop him.

**You will need**

- *Supporting facts*, *Presentation evaluation* and *Between sessions (non-fiction)* Photocopy Masters for Year 6/P7

## Before reading

- Ask the children to list the conventions and features of non-fiction texts. Do all non-fiction books have the same features?
- Ask the group to flick quickly through the book. Do the children think this text is a non-fiction book? Challenge the group to justify their answers.

**Assessment point**

Can the children use quotations and text references to support ideas and arguments?

- Remind the children they can use the glossary to look up any unfamiliar words.
- Using page 4 as an example, draw the group's attention to the appendices and briefly discuss their use.

## During reading

- Ask the children to read pages 2–11 independently, reminding them that pages 4–11 can be read in any order.
- Ask them to note down any words that end in *-able* or *-ible*.

## After reading

***Returning to the text***

- Discuss the ideas children collected while reading and use these to justify their opinions about the type of text this is.
- Ask the children about the purpose of the book. Has it been written to inform, to entertain, or to share a particular message?
- How do the layout, features, stylistic choices (having fictional characters present real information) support the purpose/s of the book?

**Assessment point**

Can the children identify the purpose, audience and organization of texts and evaluate the success of each of these elements?

### Developing comprehension

- Ask the children to locate and describe one fact or idea that particularly interested them. Is it fact or opinion? How do they know?
- Explain how the text uses real facts to support the arguments it makes. In pairs, children can use the *Supporting facts* Photocopy Master to locate key information that supports Ant's arguments.

### The author's craft

- Ask the children to look at the appendices. Why has the author placed this information here rather than in the body of the text? How does this affect how you read the book?

**Assessment point**
Can the children give detailed insight into how the structural choices support the writer's theme or purpose?

### Developing grammar, punctuation and spelling

- Look at the words ending *-able* or *-ible* (e.g. *enjoyable*, *terrible*). Explain the spelling rules when choosing which ending to use. If when the suffix is removed a root word is left, e.g. enjoy, then *-able* should be added. If not, add *-ible*, e.g. *terrible*. (There are exceptions to these rules, e.g. *sensible*.)

**Prior to Session 2**

- Ask the children to read pages 12–17 independently.
- Ask them to note down suggestions for how to conserve water, paying attention to the Collector's pages as well as Ant's.

# Session 2 (pages 18–23)

## Before reading

- Discuss the children's ideas from independent reading. Talk about how the Collector's pages are useful sources of information, but the reader needs to infer the information about conserving water, i.e. – do the opposite of what the Collector suggests.

## During reading

- Ask the children to read pages 18–23 independently.
- As they read, ask the children to list any words containing hyphens.

> **Assessment point**
> Can the children read a range of level-appropriate texts fluently and accurately?

## After reading

***Returning to the text***

Ask the children:

- Why are rainforests being cut down or set on fire? **(inferring, synthesizing)**
- How can people reduce the destruction of rainforests? Which strategies will have the biggest impact? **(recall, drawing conclusions, determining importance)**

> **Assessment point**
> Can the children clearly identify and retrieve relevant points and key ideas from different points in a text and across a range of texts?

### *Developing comprehension*

- Ask the children to look back through the book at the 'Agent Action' boxes. What is the effect of the statement 'No action required'? (People are contributing to these problems already.) Why has the author chosen to present the destruction of the environment in a positive way (i.e. through the Collector)?
- Ask the children to choose one section from the book that particularly interested them and prepare a one-minute presentation to their partner. Their partner can provide feedback on content, using *Presentation evaluation* Photocopy Master.

> **Assessment point**
> Can the children combine information with increasing precision to produce meaningful information?

### *The author's craft*

- Can the children recognize how the author uses different tones and 'voices' for the Collector and Ant? Can they identify words and phrases where the Collector is gloating that his plan is succeeding?

## Developing grammar, punctuation and spelling

- Ask the children to find 'Cuban-mahagany desk' on page 18. Ask them what it means. Does it mean the same thing without the hyphen? Explain how Cuban-mahogany desk means a desk that that has been made out of a wood grown in Cuba. Without the hyphen it would mean the desk was from Cuba and made out of mahogany but not necessarily that the wood was from Cuba.

**Prior to Session 3**

- Ask the children to read pages 26–33 independently.
- Ask them to complete *Between sessions (non-fiction)* Photocopy Master answering the comprehension questions.

# Session 3 (pages 34 and 35)

## Before reading

- As a group, share responses to comprehension questions from the children's independent reading.
- Ask the children to discuss the section that interested them most from the book so far. Why did they find it engaging? Was it the content, the author's presentation or a combination of the two? **(recall, summarizing)**

**Assessment point**

Can the children discuss the range of organizational features used and how they contribute to the overall effect of the text?

## During reading

- Ask the children to read pages 34 and 35 independently.
- Ask them to skim through the book, thinking about what the author's viewpoint is on environmental issues.

## After reading

***Returning to the text***

- As a group, discuss how the author has been creative with the conventions of non-fiction while still communicating factual information. Can the children reach a conclusion about whether this book is non-fiction or fiction?

### *Developing comprehension*

- Ask the children to share their ideas about what the author's viewpoint is on environmental issues. How effective were the book's features in achieving this?
- Discuss what the effect is of the author presenting the Collector's 'opinions' on environmental issues alongside Ant's. How might the Collector's secret plans appeal to someone less interested in environmental issues?

**Assessment point**

Can the children clearly identify and explain the writer's viewpoint, making references to the text?

## Follow-up

*Writing activities*

- Choose one environmental issue from the book and write fact sheet explaining the issue. **(short writing task)**
- Write a presentation on climate change or wild places. **(longer writing task)**

*Other literacy activities*

- As a group, write the script to a radio programme about deforestation using information from the book.
- Use one of the appendices to create a new page for the book. Can the children present the information in the style of the book, using Ant and the Collector's voices?

*Cross-curricular activities*

- Research the conservation of endangered animals, identifying what scientists do to increase their survival. **(Science)**
- Use maps, diagrams and aerial photographs to create a presentation about the rainforest bio-dome the Collector plans to build. **(Geography)**

# Space Holidays and other freaky futures

BY PAUL MASON

## Curricula correlation

### English National Curriculum

| | |
|---|---|
| Spoken language | Ask relevant questions to extend their understanding and knowledge |
| Word reading | Apply their knowledge of root words, prefixes and suffixes (morphology and etymology), both to read aloud and to understand the meaning of new words that they meet |
| Comprehension | Ask questions to improve their understanding of a text |
| | Identify how language, structure and presentation contribute to meaning |
| | Identify and discuss themes and conventions in and across a wide range of writing |
| | Distinguish between statements of fact and opinion |

***Developing grammar, punctuation, vocabulary and spelling***

| | | |
|---|---|---|
| Grammar and Punctuation | Punctuation of bullet points to list information | |
| Vocabulary and Spelling | Use of the hyphen to avoid ambiguity and other purposes | computer-atoms, 3-D, full-body |
| | Use the first letters of a word to check spelling or meaning in a dictionary | |
| | Challenge and context words | bacteria, bamboozle, claytronic, colony, cosmonaut, futurist, implant, malfunction, microprocessor, miniaturize, nanobots, nutrients, organism, phosphate, prosthetic, purification, retina, thermal |

***Reading assessment points***

| | |
|---|---|
| Word reading | Can the children read a range of level-appropriate texts fluently and accurately? |
| Comprehension | Can the children identify the purpose, audience and organization of different non-fiction texts and evaluate the success of each of these elements? |
| | Can the children explain in detail how the author has used different language features? |
| | Can the children reflect on the wider consequences or significance of information, ideas or events on the text as a whole? |
| | Can the children securely make deductions, firmly rooted in the evidence in the text? |
| | Can the children clearly identify and explain the writer's viewpoint, making reference to the text? |

## Scottish Curriculum for Excellence

| | |
|---|---|
| Listening and talking objectives | I can recognise how the features of spoken language can help in communication, and I can use what I learn ENG 2-03a |
| Reading objectives | Through developing my knowledge of context clues, punctuation, grammar and layout, I can read unfamiliar texts with increasing fluency, understanding and expression ENG 2-12a / ENG 3-12a / ENG 4-12a |
| | To show my understanding across different areas of learning, I can identify and consider the purpose and main ideas of a text and use supporting detail LIT 2-16a |
| | To help me develop an informed view, I can identify and explain the difference between fact and opinion, recognise when I am being influenced, and have assessed how useful and believable my sources are LIT 2-18a |

## Welsh National Literacy Framework

| | |
|---|---|
| Speaking | Express issues and ideas clearly, using specialist vocabulary and examples |
| Listening | Respond to others with questions and comments which focus on reasons, implications and next steps |
| Collaboration and discussion | Follow up points in group discussions, showing agreement or disagreement giving reasons |
| Reading strategies | Use a range of strategies for finding information, e.g. skimming for gist, scanning for detail |
| Comprehension | Infer ideas which are not explicitly stated, e.g. writers' viewpoints or attitudes |
| Response and analysis | Collate and make connections, e.g. prioritising, categorising, between information and ideas from different sources |

## Northern Ireland Curriculum

| | |
|---|---|
| Talking and Listening | Share, respond to and evaluate ideas, arguments and points of view and use evidence or reason to justify opinions, actions or proposals |
| Reading | Consider, interpret and discuss texts, exploring the ways in which language can be manipulated in order to affect the reader or engage attention |
| | Reconsider their initial response to texts in the light of insight and information which emerge subsequently from their reading |

# Session I (pages 2–II)

**About this book**

The world is changing and technology is developing just as fast. This book considers the latest predictions for the future, based on the most exciting advances in technology.

**You will need**

- *Between sessions (non-fiction)* and *Quiz* Photocopy Masters for Year 6/P7

## Before reading

- Look at the front cover as a group. Ask the children what kind of a book this is. What might they expect to find in a non-fiction text? Challenge children to comment on features (index, glossary); ways of presenting information (graphs or charts); content (facts and statistics); language and tone (specialist language or a formal tone?). **(predicting)**
- Read pages 2 and 3 together. How would they describe the tone of the book (warm, chatty, colloquial)? How does this compare with their expectations? **(activating and building on prior knowledge)**
- Remind the children they can use the glossary to look up any unfamiliar words.

## During reading

- Ask the children to skim pages 3–II independently. Ask them to choose two sections that interest them and to read these carefully.
- As they read, ask them to make a list of words containing hyphens and words ending with *-ough*.

## After reading

***Returning to the text***

- Ask the group to share the pages that interested them most and why they chose these pages. **(recall, personal response)**

### *Developing comprehension*

- Ask the children if they think this book has been written for a particular purpose. Is it trying to convey a message? Is it effective in doing this?
- Do the children think this book is aimed at any particular audience? Discuss how the layout of information and the tone suggests it is, asking children to find evidence.

**Assessment point**

Can the children identify the purpose, audience and organization of different non-fiction texts and evaluate the success of each of these elements?

### *Developing grammar, punctuation and spelling*

- Ask the children to give examples of the hyphenated words they found. Using examples from pages 5–11, discuss how they are used to avoid ambiguity (*computer-atoms*), add additional information (*full-body*), and to make comments about the text *3-D* (p7); *top-secret* (p9); *super-thin* (p10), etc.
- Ask children to share the *-ough* words they found and to list them according to the sound of their endings, e.g. *thought/s; although, though; enough; through*.

**Prior to Session 2**

- Ask the children to read the sections they skimmed over in depth and to read up to page 19 independently.
- As they are reading, ask the children to think about whether the author has a particular view of the future. Ask them to collect words and phrases that support their opinion.

# Session 2 (pages 20–27)

## Before reading

- Discuss the author's view about the future, using their notes.

## During reading

- Ask the children to read either the section on robots (pages 20–23) or on food (pages 24–27) independently.
- Ask the children to consider whether they agree with the probability ratings.

**Assessment point**

Can the children read a range of level-appropriate texts fluently and accurately?

## After reading

### *Returning to the text*

- As a group, discuss the ratings given. Do they agree those with the highest ratings (lab-grown meat) are the most likely and those with the lowest (robot rebellion) are the least likely? How convincing is the information that supports them? Is it the clearest way to convey the information?

### *Developing comprehension*

- Re-read pages 24 and 25. Does the author present a balanced argument about lab-grown meat? If not, which side does he favour? Challenge children to justify their opinions with evidence from the text.

**Assessment point**
Can the children clearly identify and explain the writer's viewpoint, making reference to the text?

- In pairs, give each child one side of the argument about lab-grown meat (for and against) and ask them to present their case before responding to their partner. Bring the class back together – what is the consensus?

### *The author's craft*

- Allocate each member of the group a different page and ask them to look at the language used. What is the balance between formal, technical language and informal, chatty language? Why has the author chosen to include more informal language? Does this informal tone diminish the impact of the data or weaken his argument? Challenge children to link their ideas back to audience and purpose.

**Assessment point**
Can the children explain in detail how the author has used different language features?

**Prior to Session 3**

- Ask the children to read pages 28–35 independently.
- Ask them to complete *Between sessions (non-fiction)* Photocopy Master answering the comprehension questions about the future.

# Session 3 (pages 36–38)

## Before reading

- Ask the children to share their responses to *Between sessions (non-fiction)* and discuss any misconceptions.

## During reading

- Ask the children to read pages 36 and 37 independently.
- As they read, ask them to list any new words they encounter.

## After reading

***Returning to the text***

- What was the *Jupiter Effect?* **(recall)**
- Who was George Wald? What did he predict? What do you think about his prediction? **(recall, inferring, personal response)**

### *Developing comprehension*

- Ask the children how having the 'Future bloopers' section might change how a reader thinks about the rest of the book? How does it support the informal (and sometimes light-hearted) tone the author has used to describe some future technological advancements? If this section appeared at the very beginning, what effect do they think it would have on the reader?

**Assessment point**
Can the children reflect on the wider consequences or significance of information, ideas or events on the text as a whole?

- As a group, list all the future advances in the book. Each child can choose the one they feel is most likely to be a blooper and the group can debate these. Challenge the children to use evidence from the text and their own ideas to justify their choice. **(deducting, inferring, personal response)**

**Assessment point**
Can the children securely make deductions, firmly rooted in the evidence in the text?

- Ask the children, in pairs, to read the quiz on page 38, asking and answering the questions. Do they agree with the perfect future that's suggested? **(personal response)**

### Developing vocabulary

- What new words have the children learned from reading this book? If they were preparing a glossary for a younger group of children, which additional words would they include? Working in pairs, list new words and use a dictionary to write definitions.

## Follow-up

*Writing activities*

- Write a new section for the book about a possible future advance the children have invented themselves. **(longer writing task)**
- Write a diary or blog entry for a child living in the future. **(shorter writing task)**

*Other literacy activities*

- Work in pairs to devise quiz questions about one section of the book using the *Quiz* Photocopy Master. Ask pairs to swap their quiz sheet with one on another section. Pairs can read the new section, answering the questions on their quiz sheet.
- As a class, debate the question: Will life be better in the year 2100?

*Cross-curricular activities*

- Imagine it is the year 2315 and the technological advances described in this book are now out-dated! Use found materials to make a model of one piece of technology for display in the local museum. Write notes to accompany it, describing what it is and what it used to do. **(DT)**
- Use the Internet to research other possible future advances. Make an interactive poster to explain one of them to other class members. **(DT/Computing)**